SCORPIONICA

SCORPIONICA

KARYNA McGLYNN

NEW MICHIGAN PRESS
TUCSON, ARIZONA

NEW MICHIGAN PRESS
8058 E. 7TH ST
TUCSON, AZ 85710

<http://newmichiganpress.com/nmp>

Orders and queries to nmp@thediagram.com.

ISBN 978-1-934832-43-1. SECOND EDITION.

Printed in the United States of America.

Design by Ander Monson.

Cover image by Leigh Prather | Dreamstime.com.

CONTENTS

ANIMALS GOING TO HELL

Quiver gentle over their sins,
taste the spring melt.

Nothing on the television
about taboos or the mongrels
which are unto our city—

Who is
letting you go, ma chienne?
Where will you crawl to die?

The blossoms
on the tomato-plants are falling
fast this year, only June now.

This morning here, a little girl
came into our kitchen,
a rifle through her empty leash.

BEFORE ANYTHING HAPPENED THE HOUSE HAD NO SKELETON

the termites had deboned the thing
it was clean there was no saving it

in one bedroom a dresser with blue drawers
its peg-legs rested on pure membrane

a girl just stood in her underwear
ran the tips of her fingers over her ribs

thought *greyhound* no one knew no explaining
why she didn't fall through the floor

the kids were drinking beer in the yard
the tetherball rope caught one girl's throat

her mother's face obscured
behind the porch screen the mesquite shadow

no one could make her out
her feet rested on hot sashes of dust

the sounds on the television were far away
as that big caliche mound looked like a waving man

the president got shot
the boards stayed together for another three days

it was a matter of apathy or swelling
or everyone was too hot to move

PHOTO

My mother stands next to the lake, shouldering a shotgun.
It's late summer in Texas—
her eyes are closed and she is laughing—
a piece of long hair, electric, caught in her mouth.
Wind off the water pulls the green dress taut.

She's 20 and tiny—you would think that she's joking,
holding a basketball in her underwear band,
a motorcycle helmet, a balloon, anything
but a child. Being poor and uncomfortably hot
are the worst things that have happened to her.

I want to untangle myself from that dress,
drop to her feet, naked and complete,
brush through the sand around her, insist:
Listen, I saw it first-hand.
There is a knotted, poisonous place inside his testicles.
When I'm born, he will die.

But flushed with heat and possibility,
she is hoping for a boy and hasn't yet heard
the news about Elvis. She laughs,
aims level into the green distance.

I ask the elastic to snap.
I want to bounce out, past my father's bare feet,
off the limestone ledge—
I want to leave them alone on this shore,
waving, one less problem between them.

She looks at my father and nestles her finger
against the lazy curve of the trigger, the open "C"—
It's so easy, I want to tell her.
Shoot! Do it now! Quick, before I change my mind.

Her bones jerk. The shutter snaps.
There is a white explosion in the August air.
A duck collapses, neck-first into the dark water
where three others take to sudden, silent flight.
Her surprised laugh, wild, resounds.
My father smiles, lowers the camera, falters.

SCORPIONICA

This is how it started: honeysuckles insinuated
into my mouth. The pecan trees grew a hot ruff
of fungus. I grew fat as a larva; I couldn't breathe.

My mother then: so young and consummate,
I can't possibly belong to her. She, too, is a baby.
She has no third eye. Her forehead is clear

gelatin absence where a spoon has dislodged Mick,
my father, flicked him out like a cancerous wafer,
refilled the skin to begin again. She stands in the room,

an oscillating fan: cool head on a thin spine,
shaking slow, shuddering inwardly in infinite
disapproval. This world of men guilty until proven

otherwise. I admire this trait immensely.
I figure and refill with figure, words looping
their long unfinished tails along my lips.

I can never sleep. The house, white as lime,
has burned twice before. Bougainvilleas flare outside
my bedroom, tornados funnel down from nowhere.

They begin in my ear. Here, the yard is littered
with coral snakes; when I find them, they are already
severed with a hoe, sometimes in half, or smaller hunks

of snake long dead, milky eyes filmed in
forgotten languor. But why is it, whoever keeps
killing these snakes has forgotten the rhyme

inculcate: red on yellow, kill a fellow,
    red on black, my friend Jack,
        black on red, my friend Fred.

These truncations are always Freds and Jacks,
Freds and Jacks interrupted mid-'s' in their slither,
liver sliced where they wriggled through the beans.

Do snakes have livers? Do the venomous ones go free?
Back up slow when you hear a rattle. Snakes are blind, but
they can smell you with their tongues. What does this mean?

I run through the sticky grass because it cuts
and clings to my legs. I understand the candid
smell of men and know down in the salt of me

I will love them more than women, who are
unpredictable, who say things pale and sideways,
who drop just out of sight in the side-pockets

and try to remove me, piece by piece; my tiny teeth
honeypocked, bought, tucked in a pillow; birthmark
trisected like a strawberry, eaten away by knives:

lunar calendar on the wane. My name a dangling
modifier, no recognizable forebear, head severed
from meaning; one day replaced with six flinty

pointing parts, impossible to drawl, lose, or cuddle.
My chin accretes suddenly, coins in a bank, stalwart.
Now I am decisive and trustworthy. Don't smirk.

This is how it started: this apricot child in heavy syrup.
Heat. I wondered, is the world nothing but strife?
Is there no relief? Yes, respite when I'm finished. Then.

I am outfitted for battle, little scorpion whirring
and hissing in the cool olive water, going click, prick,
wending its fast white death. My tolerance for death

is immense, a giant fish which moves in my saliva,
dilates my mind, devours my body. I come
from a hot and lazy world. I fight back the thick of it

like drugged wool. I cauterize my leaking memory
with a red pincer, weave a yellow jacket nest crisp
around my soft parts. Red and yellow kill a fellow.

Weakness is the worst fate. Venom wriggles away,
an unimpeded body coiled in the cool greens.
What was I saying? If I open my mouth too wide

I will accidentally swallow womankind like a bird egg.
My lover insinuates himself in my mouth, he's fixed
the rhythm. Don't move, he says, I'm trying to love you.

EARLY CHILDHOOD

The buck my uncles shot hung skinless,
back hoofs hooked to the porch rafters,
the outstretched tongue a dark spigot for the blood-drain—
a place where every shed and tractor tire palmed
a sleeping snake, where my life was as shallow
as the beam of a flashlight—
        and it was all *batteries, batteries*
that lit up my yellow marrow in the yard,
where dreams of orange extension cords
uncoiled to pull their long necessary bodies
through the scrub,
        the ashy sinisia, the pipes
where toothed cables surfaced slick
from sinks and toilets—every appliance
growing mucous and mutinous in the night,
coiling round the chest of my stiff cot,
gripping it like a grounded quail.
It was a rough grotto beneath
the sycophantic sweet-heat of fig tree
        where I listened
to the progress of the day's wide, wet mouth
lapping at its night wounds, where the yard darkened
with the smell of frying venison
        and *the batteries, the batteries*
and all the bloody gullet
of couched uncles suddenly up
from bourbon naps and billiards, their sunburned
chests bellowing for all the world *where are you*
        and *who will fetch a switch?*

AMANDA HOPPER'S HOUSE

It was a farmhouse for killing,
    the kind I saw in the paper above a row of senior portraits:

girls found in the basement.
    Frosted eye-shadow, bangs like birds' nests.

Girls I saw and said to myself:
    good. they deserve it.

'The stupid *sluts'* sit on my tongue.
    I swallow, but the stupid sluts stick there like chicken bones.

Like Amanda's older sister Gloria,
    splayed across the hood of her boyfriend's Chevy Nova.

From the breakfast table
    we watch him open her dry skinny legs and press

his belt buckle into her denim crotch.
    It's 9 am and they chew grape gum.

We follow the unfurling snail silhouettes of their French kisses
    as Mrs. Hopper looks out, wary, from behind

the newspaper headline: *Body of Missing Teen Found in Family Shed.*
    She fishes in her pink robe for a pack of cigarettes,

places a menthol between her feathering lips,
    flicks her lighter, picks her cuticle,

tells us out the corner of her mouth
    to stop gaping and eat our fucking Lucky Charms.

THE MEN OF CAMP MYSTIC

We knew, intimately, the location of every penis
on the grounds of Camp Mystic for Girls—
each man a burning "Y" beneath our eyelids.

We knew, without looking, the exact shape of the boy
scooping hard maple ice cream, and the pleated sound
of the Director approaching in his soft loafers.

We jackknifed into the Guadalupe,
asses thrust high for the arborist who, we knew,
sat watching in the walnut tree with giant clippers.

Even the old gatekeeper in his limestone hovel—
we saw him sip whiskey in the TV's blue bath
and knew that *he had one.*

We thrilled, secretly, over that tenured skin,
the mailman's rounds, the doctor called in for fractures,
heat stroke, fat ticks hooked in our skin.

Those men and boys who would not speak to us,
or *could not,* who blushed fierce in August labor
and became small gods in their enforced silence,

their down-turned eyes—pimply boys gone Byronic
under our constant gaze, those giant Southern lawns
littered with lounging sirens in bright plastic shorts.

I mean: we sharpened our nails and teeth on the porch posts,
swaggered round the flagpole, hands on hearts
in the swell of Kate Smith's wavering bosom.

But then, when a man passed, we stripped the weakest,
offered her up for inspection, shoved her struggling body
into the full heat of noon, rollicked in the violence

of her sublime embarrassment—not one of us blinking
but waiting our turn as we glared out at our bait
from some rare & temporal patch of shade.

PARENTS' DAY

Defecting from the potato salad
my mother & I saw this prehistoric bird

(and all the while this unseen leech
siphoned her blood like a cherry phosphate)

The bird wasn't a heron
but a bigger blue
a silent thing which winged through the corridor
of river oak & black snake

We wiped the coleslaw's white from our lips
and said *oh, hello*
wet hair combed into discreet honeybuns

And my mother's leech just ladled her up
in the lawn mill of Laura Ashley bleach
& red-faced men with meaty manicures
cologne boiling in each pore

while somewhere the great thing wended
and we in some weird social guilt
shifted from sandal to sandal and said
we were the only ones who saw it
and who *said* that we saw it

WHEREVER A GIRL'S BEEN GROUNDED

I close her pressboard door, click the flimsy lock,
pull a nightgown over her tartan skirt, baby-T, padded bra.

I prepare the minutiae of her escape: ball-up her stockings,
shove an ATM card down her underwear, spit in her palms.

I look up into the endless white climb of her closet,
test the strength of the shelves, give her a leg up.

Now she crowns through the floor of her attic,
surprised by the ease with which all gives way above her—

See how she dives up through the dark scuttle-hole:
upward dog, rising star, toe-to-toe, head low.

Pink meadows of insulation stretch from the crossbeam.
She hears her parents' huge bodies shift in the king-sized bed.

I tranquilize the dog, as, somewhere over the garage,
she unfolds a ladder quiet as hair and stops to listen

mid-flight: a gecko frozen in the sudden porch light.
My chest floods with false alarm but, quick as anything,

she slithers under the lip of the carport and out
into that dwindling *yes*, some lovely old black night.

SUBURBAN BARBARISM

Loose, the violent bulls-eye genitals
of overblown poppies, bloody dinner plate
lofted and smashed on the lawn's clipped edge,
the violence makes a different sound here:
Easter egg trod upon by patent leather shoes,
horse hoof stepping delicately through a skull,
a barbarism which breeds in treeless back-lots,
the wild hedges pushing, insisting, welling
black and viscous from the spidery spigot,
from the cul-de-sacs built and left bare, bricks
piled but not laid, haunted with half-empty
bottles of cinnamon liquor and torn panties,
night sites of bonfires, fireworks and dark cars
where god knows, god knows, dead coyotes
and headless Barbie-dolls walk upright
through the smooth unpeopled streets.

POST 11TH BIRTHDAY

The cat ambles in and out of frame.
Someone picks up the camera, sets it down;
the frame jogs twice. Then they're laughing.
They've just discovered: my party was a silent movie
but who's to blame for forgetting to check the volume?
Briefly, they consider calling me back:
rewrap the presents, relight the candles.
No, it's just too silly and I'm not a good enough actress.

They break into the Jack Daniels
he lies about his age more than once, speaks in Cajun French,
shows off his muscles, accuses my mother
of buying him presents that are really for her.
Shot of the wok, shot of the blender, they get drunk.

My voice is faint off-camera: *Coke! Coke!*
My mother slurs back: *Not now—I'm a film director!*
He pretends to cook a roux,
puts a frozen egg-roll in his pants pocket.
My mother goes *ooooohhh, baby*
but in the end, it's my fault—
my incessant demand for cola cuts things short
just as they begin to get interesting.

My mother's hand descends over the camera lens,
a slow-mo jellyfish. He grabs it by the wrist—
it curls up like something stunned.
No, he says, *not like that.*

GREY LIGHT RAN ALONG THE SCALLOPS OF THIS DREAM

where my father, dead for 12 years
called down the hallway *everybody inside*

there was thunder in the distance
I thought of his innocuous decree

his voice struck tin then and there
the hall was a storm drain

I ran out next to the pool with knives
I tried to find an outlet to wedge them in

I found an oven in the shed, in the pool
dead leaves circled like wagons

DIXON HANGING

Because I found my dyslexic cousin
hanging from the tree branch like a dead "J"

    my childhood is overdue—
    it blows like a black sweater

against the storm shutters. I fall in love
with men whose heads are twisting

    hornets hives—their mouths
    steep in open mason jars.

My legs are tea towels, long blue slings.
Dixon fills them with flat river stones,
winds his freckled arm in violence:

    The hill country hears you, honey,
    it will weave you into its hot nest.

Home lords its blasted center over you—
pulls its heft up the spine, that salty rope.

    Your past piles up ramshackle,
    a long grain elevator. I can see

Dixon's tongue flapping against that tin
like an orange flag—eyes corrugated

    ankles tagged with burr.
    Down there, somewhere,

a front door propped open with a cinderblock.
Screen like a sieve, sticky with wasp wings.
Inside, someone always hums

    hoards black-tooth combs to tame
    a cousin's slender curling neck.

UPON HEARING YOUR GOOD NEWS, I THOUGHT

You *would*. I'm older, true,
but you've always done the growing-up things first:
kiss, man, blood, funny cigarette, piss on the stick,
already painting a big blue window.

Remember the yellow water-snake?
Unstuffed from your stocking,
it poured and poured out of itself—
we couldn't keep hold.
It was commedia dell' arte in our bedroom,
that condom-banana combo flying,
flogging the air, that old miser.
And then it got stiff and bruised,
a dirty cab color with our fingerprints
where we couldn't leave it alone,
and we left it in a drawer then.
It sealed itself against the wood
and grew thin and eventually exploded
on our socks and underwear.
Yellow and fast, slippery Tantalus,
you sealed your thumb across the hose's copper valve
and waited for something to happen:
an impossible swelling,
an explosion in your hand.

I think of how your body will
produce a body, turn in on itself and divide
the soft core where the fingers go—
Your green eye looks up through me,
examines empty rooms and rooms and shakes

my head in gentle admonishment,
feeds me until I'm too full to breathe,
slips my hand up the happy sock-puppet
of your idiot pregnancy, caricature of womanhood:
a rose mouth in washable marker
opens and opens for air.

CROWNING

Fig. 1—The wealthy girl gives birth.
        See how the Ob-Gyn opens her thighs early,
pouring his unhurried body into the wood and yellow room.

        La: he kisses her on the mouth.

Here: my cousin blossoms beneath this
        tender hook: her body is a dust ruffle.
        Call and response: wah-wah.
        [Your baby duck is on its way].

Fig. 2—The springy arcadia of a northern university.

        Her body, my body, this big turf body.

Here, at last, symbiosis: the inexplicable bite:
someone's epidural sliding in from behind: I feel

her body quake, a wall-mounted pencil sharpener,
something a sweating child grinds into her,
pulls out:
        sharp and stinging graphite.

Fig. 3—A passing dean in his purple robes.
        See how he pulls on gloves and drives
        his hands down through my body, then

rims me on the blank stare
of an upturned dry-erase board.

Fig. 4—A southern maternity ward at lunchtime.

        The glee with which a menopausal relative rocks
        her phone, gloating over the tiny body: gray, limbless.

A prenatal complication sways in her mind like a giant piñata:
        she makes the whole room dizzy—*wah-wah*—
she glitters with panic and swings her giant empathy stick.

Fig. 5—A different view from the gurney.

        The northern sky breaks its milky water:
        over the skull: over and over: this softening

the dean smoothes the cone of my head like gray clay.

        la, he says, *maintenant.*

Fig. 6—A gushing fountain, a paddling of ducks.

        I waddle down, single-file: the swollen weight
        of this ambition,
        this crown
        and the body following suit,
        threading its exposed intestines back

onto a dark spool.
I fling my grief across the continent.

        It plinks into a pan of afterbirth:

Fig. 7—Nobody can take their eyes off it.

DIAMONDBACK RATTLER

Here: caliche path bogged with buttercup.
Here: snake feathered with his old skin.

He warns my general direction with the rasp of his rattle,

his glaucous eyes lifted.

Old belly man,

here is the biblical distance, distrust incarnate.

But who is the head?

And who the heel?

Unlike the tattoo of you
I saw torque around a lover's ankle:

fresh inked, blood pricked,
bottle-green & bruise blue,

skin and snake at once impacted—

here: you exist under a skin no longer your own.
For that: we are not so far removed.

Both relegated:
all body, all organ

which winds into itself—this unhinging entity
out for the swallow.

Our greatest prize: a whole egg.

Our enmity: a split seed on the caliche path—
a sizzling sound as the wet heat solders the old husk

back into its single self,

as your glossed diamonds slide from a dry white sleeve.

ERIN WITH THE FEATHERED HAIR

In summer, I remember where I'm from and why
my knees smell like yellow onions—
why you, Erin, are standing in my living room
straddling your brother's outgrown Huffy:
you want me back in the cul-de-sac badlands.
Your hair is fresh-feathered and you are showing off
your air-conditioned underwear, a Weiner's six-pack,
a stolen margarita lip-gloss in your snatching hand.
I know: it's hot and I never left.
You run to my closet and cut all the necks out,
never asked and never will,
would I like a red cigarette?
When no one is looking, I twist in the sheets and—
what do you think? Am I a Roxy Music album cover?
I can iron out my voice, but still,
I am field stock, body a rebar.
You wrench my freckles, my towhead out of hiding,
smearing my body in bright orange paint and profanity,
flinging open my cupboards and sneering,
What's in the shoebox? Something bad?
In the summer you unpeel my northern pretense,
leave me quivering in a glitter tube-top
as you unlock the liquor cabinet and give me the keys
to the duplex kingdom you swear is rightfully mine.

WHERE THERE SHOULD BE A PLANT STAND, THERE ISN'T

I hear people talking in the kitchen, but there's no way
to get to them; they've had three drinks too many.

The worst is my bedroom, which has been roped off
with yellow police tape. They've pulled up the carpet.

I think *someone's been here—a smoker,*
trying to bypass the now-defunct security system.

Through my window I see my sister step from her car.
She plans to confront me about the thing she can't yet know.

I slip back through the shotgun rooms, and once again
enter my mother's with its unheated waterbed.

In the left-hand drawer of her vanity, I know I can find
her expired pregnancy test with its indelible blue lines.

But, perhaps, like everything else, these are mutable details.
Shouting somewhere in the house now and I have to hurry.

If I take it out now, I might kill myself. If I leave it
I won't remember what I came here to do.

NEAR 74 RUE LAURISTON

I am a hard woman on white sheets,
by degrees unmade: ici, *pres d'ici,*
ballpeened into two-dimensions.
I feign sleep, ass-up, beneath
the bullet point of your cock.

In the night I pad quiet & pee quiet
rapt in my strange woman coat
which functions & won't stop it
like the restive lights in hotel halls
which burn, intractable, at all hours.

Don't think for a second I can't
be had so completely time recedes
to let me look back on my simple self,
its accommodation like a single room
unoccupied, heady with new blue paint.

Though—when I say I want you
I speak from inside a tricky set
of catacombs, wings, extensions
where space is wanted—there you go
I open up like heavy drapes, like this.

My lust fulfills, refills its definition—
when you call it comes out lock-step,
tilts to look on me with deep-set eyes:
Qui êtes-vous? You think you know me
born down on this bed in my likeness?

A SMOKE RING LISPS UNDER THE DOOR

When I roll over in bed, I roll over in a California king,
the wallpaper plashed with marigolds in the dark.
You have your fingers inside a little girl.

I cry out, but not for the reasons you think.
The rocking chair that smells of blackened bananas
has an unmistakable occupant now. *You cannot deny me this.*

When you kiss me it is full-cupped, public and flagrant.
You fold your loins into me in recompense for the child
who shimmies away like a little love crocodile.

When the room fills with smoke, a small hand shakes me open.
It doesn't belong to you; you sleep, not animal-like
but thanatopic, a grey shaving of something, once

so sexually resplendent, I barely recognize the skull
which lifts from my grandfather's camphory pillow, the *what is it*
that issues forth, the silvery *fire* in response.

ACKNOWLEDGMENTS

Many thanks to the editors of the following journals, where some of the poems in this collection first appeared, sometimes in earlier forms:

Cranky: "Dixon Hanging"
eratio: "Animals Going to Hell"
42opus: "Erin with the Feathered Hair"
Gulf Coast: "Crowning"
Hotel Amerika: "Early Childhood"
Indiana Review: "Diamondback Rattler"
The Pedestal Magazine: "Photo"
Stirring: "Upon Hearing Your Good News, I Thought"
Willow Springs: "The Men of Camp Mystic"

Some of the poems in this collection were included in a manuscript which won the Hopwood Award for Poetry at the University of Michigan in 2006.

A huge thank you to Michelle Brown, Bruce Covey, Linda Gregerson, Lorna Goodison, Cyan James, Marie Howe, Khaled Mattawa, Ray McDaniel, and Adam Theriault for lending their super-powers to this project.

KARYNA MCGLYNN is the author of *I Have to Go Back to 1994 and Kill a Girl*, winner of the Kathryn A. Morton Prize from Sarabande Books, and a book of flash fiction, *Alabama Steve*. Her poems have appeared in *Fence, Salt Hill, Columbia Poetry Review, Subtropics, Court Green, Ninth Letter*, and *Phoebe*. Karyna received her MFA from the University of Michigan, and is currently a PHD candidate in Literature & Creative Writing at the University of Houston. She is the Managing Editor of *Gulf Coast* and coordinator of the Houston Indie Book Fest and *Gulf Coast* Reading Series.

NEW MICHIGAN PRESS, based in Tucson, Arizona, is a small chapbook press. Together with *DIAGRAM*, NMP sponsors a yearly chapbook competition.

DIAGRAM, a journal of text, art, and schematic, is published bimonthly at THEDIAGRAM.COM. Periodic print anthologies are available from the New Michigan Press at NEWMICHIGANPRESS.COM/NMP.

COLOPHON

Text is set in a digital version of Jenson, designed by Robert Slimbach in 1996, and based on the work of punchcutter, printer, and publisher Nicolas Jenson.

www.ingramcontent.com/pod-product-compliance
Lightning Source LLC
LaVergne TN
LVHW051023080826
845145LV00009B/2766

* 9 7 8 1 9 3 4 8 3 2 4 3 1 *